W9-AVC-360

DATE DUE

DEMCO, INC. 38-2931

PERU
the people and culture

Bobbie Kalman & Tammy Everts

A Bobbie Kalman Book
The Lands, Peoples, and Cultures Series

 Crabtree Publishing Company
www.crabtreebooks.com

The Lands, Peoples, and Cultures Series

Created by Bobbie Kalman

For Robert MacGregor

Coordinating editor
Ellen Rodger

Project editor
Sean Charlebois

Production Coordinator
Rosie Gowsell

Prepress and printing
Worzalla Publishing Company

Photographs
John Curtis/Andes Press Agency: p. 22 (top); Gamma: p.11 (bottom); Gamma: p. 25 (top right); Fiona Good/South American Pictures: p. 26 (top); Anna Gordon/Andes Press Agency: p. 7 (bottom right); Kathy Jarvis/South American Pictures: p. 3, p. 6 (bottom); Bill Leimbach/South American Pictures: p. 1, p. 19; Marion Morrison/South American Pictures: p. 17 (top left); Tony Morrison/South American Pictures: p. 14 (top), p. 15 (bottom right), p. 15 (top), p. 16 (top), p. 17 (bottom), p. 18 (top), p. 19 (bottom), p. 21, p. 22 (bottom), p. 24 (top), p. 26 (bottom), p. 28 (bottom), p. 28 (top), p. 30 (top), p. 31 (top), p. 7 (bottom), p. 7 (top), p. 8 (bottom), p. 9 (top); Rex Features: p. 11 (middle); Carlos Reyes-Manzo/Andes Press Agency p. 10 (bottom), p. 10 (top), p. 14 (bottom), p. 29 (bottom); Karen Ward/South American Pictures: p. 20

Illustrations
Andy Cienik: p. 4-5
Margaret Amy Reiach: Inca *quipu*, pp. 6-11
David Wysotski, Allure Illustrations: back cover

Cover: Ancient peoples in Peru were highly skilled artisans. The face from this Nazca ceramic pot, created by the people living in the Nazca River Valley, is between 1,500 and 2,000 years old. The Nazca depicted many tasks from daily life in their art, including farming, warfare, and religion. These images have taught archaeologists a great deal about life in Peru thousands of years ago.

Title page: Peruvian music has been part of religious and public festivals, or *fiestas*, in Peru for hundreds of years. Musicians in Peru today play a combination of traditional instruments used by the Inca, and modern instruments introduced by the Spanish and other European and American settlers.

Icon: The llama is an important symbol of Peru. The ancient Andean civilizations of South America tamed llamas about 5,000 years ago to serve as pack animals, sources of food and fuel, and to offer as sacrifices to the sun god, Inti. Llamas still serve important functions in the daily lives of highland Peruvians, such as taking produce to markets.

Back cover: The Andean condor is the largest flying land bird on Earth, with a wingspan up to 12 feet (3.7 meters). Condors live and nest high in the Andes mountains of South America and soar down to the Pacific coast daily to search for food.

Published by
Crabtree Publishing Company

PMB 16A,	612 Welland Avenue	73 Lime Walk
350 Fifth Avenue	St. Catharines	Headington
Suite 3308	Ontario, Canada	Oxford OX3 7AD
New York	L2M 5V6	United Kingdom
NY 10118		

Cataloging in Publication Data
Kalman, Bobbie, 1947-
  Peru. The people and culture / Bobbie Kalman & Tammy Everts.
    p. cm. -- (Lands, peoples, and cultures series)
Includes index.
    ISBN 0-7787-9342-7 (RLB) -- ISBN 0-7787-9710-4 (PB)
1. Peru--Civilization--Juvenile literature. 2. Peru--Social life and customs--Juvenile literature. I. Everts, Tammy, 1970- II. Title. III. Series.
    F3410 .K35 2003
    985--dc21
                                    2002013918
                                    LC

Contents

Inca creation myth

Peruvians have many stories about their history. Ancient Peruvians did not have a written language, so these stories were passed down orally from one generation to the next. Since the time of the great Inca Empire, there have been several versions of a story that tells how the Earth was made and how the Inca civilization was founded. The details of the story depend on what region it is told in. Here is one version of the Inca creation **myth**.

Manco Capac and Mama Ocllo

A long time ago, the world was filled with misery and poverty, and its people were uncivilized. The great sun god, Inti, was unhappy with the world, so he sent a married brother and sister, Manco Capac and Mama Ocllo, to found a new civilization.

Manco Capac and Mama Ocllo rose out of the blue waters of Lake Titicaca high in the Andes mountains and stood on the lake's shore. Inti had given them a golden stick for testing the

surrounding land for cultivation. He had told them: "When you find a suitable place, you will found a new state and teach the people how to live proper lives, and worship me."

The journey to this new land took a long time. Manco Capac and Mama Ocllo traveled north from Lake Titicaca, through the Andes, all the way testing the land with the golden stick to see if it was suitable for the founding of the new state. Eventually, they reached the lovely Cuzco Valley. Manco Capac took the golden stick and placed it in the ground and saw it disappear. He turned to Mama Ocllo and said, "The land here is suitable for growing crops. We can now carry out the mission that Inti has asked of us."

The city of Cuzco and the Inca state was founded that day in the name of Inti the sun god. The Sun Temple was built in Cuzco and Manco Capac became the first Inca ruler.

Manco Capac taught his people to cultivate and **irrigate** the land. Mama Ocllo taught the women spinning, weaving, and sewing. The descendants of Manco Capac came to be called by the name of Hanan Cuzco, or High Cuzco, and the relatives of Mama Ocllo were known as Hurin Cuzco, or Lower Cuzco.

Early civilizations

People have lived in what is now Peru for at least 12,000 years. **Archaeologists** believe the first communities were located along the coast. The inhabitants of these villages depended on fishing and farming for food. Over the centuries, several civilizations emerged in Peru, adapting to life at high altitudes, in coastal deserts, and in the tropical jungle. Some of the earliest civilizations were the Chavin, Nazca, Moche, Huari, and Chimu.

A warrior image carved in stone at Cerro Sechin is 3,000 years old.

The Chavin

The Chavin civilization lived in the northern highlands and coastal areas of Peru between 950 B.C. and 450 B.C. The ruins of a large Chavin temple can be found north of Lima in the town of Chavin de Huantar. The Chavin believed this temple was the center of the universe, and they performed many religious rites and ceremonies there.

The Nazca

The Nazca people lived in the southern coastal desert of Peru from 200 B.C. to 600 A.D. They were great astronomers and mathematicians. They used this knowledge to build networks of aqueducts to **divert** water running down from the mountains. The water created **oases** in the desert that allowed the Nazca people to grow crops.

In the 1930s, people flying in planes above the desert near the village of Nazca noticed hundreds of lines, pictures of animals, birds, and other shapes etched in the *pampa*, or desert sand. Some of the images are up to 985 feet (300 meters) long and some straight lines stretch for miles. No one knows the purpose of these shapes and lines, or geoglyphs. Following a flood and an earthquake, which occurred sometime after 300 A.D., the Nazca abandoned their cities, burying them in the sand before they left.

The Moche

The Moche people lived in the valleys of the Moche and Chicama rivers in northern Peru from 100 to 700 A.D. They fished the waters of the Pacific and farmed in desert fields. The Moche developed irrigation systems for

(above) The New Temple at Chavin de Huantar, in the north, influenced architecture as far south as Lake Titicaca.

bringing water from the Andes to the dry coastal region. They were accomplished farmers who grew avocados, corn, peanuts, beans, and squash. At their capital city they built two flat-topped pyramids, the Pyramid of the Sun and the Pyramid of the Moon. The pyramids were central to Moche religion and government. The Moche were also skilled potters. Their artisans recorded wars and daily life on the pottery they made. Moche pottery also depicts weaving techniques, hunting, and cooking. Members of the Moche middle class lived in clay and wood structures, while priests and warriors were part of an upper class, and lived closest to the large ceremonial pyramids and other temples.

The Huari

At its greatest strength, around 800 A.D., the Huari Empire stretched from the Ocoña valley in the south to Cajamarca in the north. The Huari were a warrior society from near today's city of Ayacucho. They conquered nearby people and adopted the religion of the Aymara people of neighboring Bolivia around 600 A.D.

(above) At Pikillacta, near Cuzco, an example of Huari architecture lies in ruin.

The Chimu

The Chimu lived on the northern coast of Peru from 1150 to 1470 A.D. They were skilled potters, weavers, and metalworkers. The Chimu built irrigation systems for their crops, with the longest canal extending 20 miles (32 kilometers) from the Chicam Valley to the capital city of Chan Chan. The Chimu were great city builders. Chan Chan is believed to have had a population of 100,000 and stretched over 52 square miles (20 square kilometers). The Chimu were conquered by the Incas in 1476 and absorbed into the Inca Empire.

(below) The Nazcas made ceramic pots decorated with multi-colored faces. This painted Nazca pot is between 1,500 and 2,000 years old.

(below) The ruins of the Chimu capital of Chan Chan, which was once home to 100,000 people. The dry climate of the coastal region has helped preserve the ancient city, which is located near the modern city of Trujillo.

The Inca Empire

The Inca was once the largest civilization in South America. The Incas lived in the Cuzco region of Peru as early as the 1100s, but historians have recorded 1438 as the beginning of their empire. From 1438 to 1532, the Incas expanded their empire across Peru. They were conquered by the Spanish in 1532. The Incas were the most powerful civilization in Peru for less than one hundred years, but they made a lasting impression in that short period.

Origins and expansion

Originally "Inca" was the family name of the rulers who lived in the Cuzco region of Peru, high in the Andes mountains. The Inca called themselves *Tawantinsuyu*. In the 1100s, the founder of the Inca dynasty, Manco Capac, led his people to the site of the present-day city of

Cuzco, and it became their capital. In the 1300s, under their fourth ruler, or Inca, Mayta Capac, they expanded their territory. As the Inca Empire grew, neighboring **cultures** and peoples were absorbed. When the Spanish arrived in the 1520s, the Inca controlled more than one-third of South America, with a population of nine to sixteen million people under their rule.

The Sapa Inca

The ruler of the Inca people was called the "Sapa Inca," meaning "only emperor." The Sapa Inca's subjects believed that this ruler was god on Earth because he was descended from the sun god, Inti. The Sapa Inca's word was law. No ordinary woman was thought good enough to be his queen, so the Sapa Inca married his eldest sister, who was another descendant of the sun god. She was called the *Coya*. The Sapa Inca had over one hundred "secondary wives."

Inca society

Inca society was based on sharing. People did not work for money. The goods they produced were distributed as people needed them. Young couples received a house and some land for farming. For each child born, they were given more land. Children helped in the fields and at home. Older people were given tasks such as collecting firewood and teaching the children. After a lifetime of working, elderly Incas were provided with food and clothing.

The Inca were skilled artisans and their art depicts images of battles they won as they spread their empire across what is now Peru.

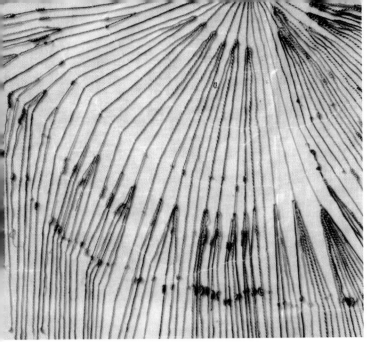

The Incas used a **quipu,** *a two-foot-long counting device with wool threads, to keep detailed records.*

Keeping records

The Incas had no written system for recording information. Instead, they used a *quipu*, which was a network of different-colored strings. The colors of the strings and the number and position of knots along the strings recorded the goods and people in each city.

Religious beliefs

The Inca believed in gods who represented the different parts of nature. The most important nature god was the sun god, Inti. Every Inca city had a large carved stone, called an Intihuatana, that marked the days the sun passed directly overhead at noon. On these days, festivals were held to thank Inti for providing light. Llamas, guinea pigs, and, occasionally, humans were sacrificed to Inti.

Viracocha, the Creator, ruled over the gods. Some Inca legends say he has left the Earth, but will one day return.

The Incas also believed that certain places and objects were inhabited by supernatural forces.

These holy sites, called *huacas*, included temples, tombs, hills, natural springs, and caves. Some spirits were also thought to live in plants. Inca healers used these herbs to treat illness.

End of the Empire

The Inca Empire came to an end soon after the Spanish arrived. In the 1520s, Francisco Pizarro, a Spanish explorer, came to Peru in search of gold. He captured the Inca ruler Atahualpa in 1533 and held him for ransom. Gold was collected from all corners of the empire to provide for Atahualpa's release, but once Pizarro received the ransom, he killed Atahualpa and put a new ruler in his place. This new ruler did what the Spanish wanted. At first, he helped the Spanish crush Inca rebellions, but later led his own rebellion, which the Spanish ended after a fierce battle. Other rebellions were unsuccessful and the Spanish became the new rulers of the Inca Empire.

The fortress of Sacsayhuaman was the Inca's most impressive structure. The Inca were able to inflict heavy losses on the Spanish invaders before being captured and executed in a rebellion.

For nearly 300 years the Spanish controlled Peru. They took over much of Peru's farmlands and resources of gold and silver. The Spanish forced the indigenous peoples to work on Spanish farms and in their mines. The Spanish also brought African slaves and, later, Asian laborers to Peru. Millions of people died in the Spanish silver mines, and most farm workers were treated poorly.

did not help the majority of Peruvians. Most of Peru's wealth was in the hands of just a few people.

Toward independence

Indigenous Peruvians fought to regain their freedom in 1780, when Tupac Amaru II led an Inca uprising against the Spanish rulers. About 60,000 indigenous people took control of southern Peru. Tupac was eventually captured, taken to Cuzco, and tortured and executed by the Spanish. In the 1820s, there was another uprising, this time aided by troops from Argentina led by General Jose de San Martin, who had defeated the Spanish forces in Chile. Peruvians were also aided by the army of Simon Bolivar, a general from Venezuela who helped many South American countries gain independence from Spain. Peru was declared independent on July 28, 1821, and by 1826 the last Spanish troops in Peru had surrendered.

Years of conflict

The young nation of Peru faced many difficulties, including fighting among military leaders, called *caudillos*, who fought each other for control of the country. Severe poverty and war with neighboring countries also caused problems for Peru through the 1800s. Near the end of the 1800s, foreign companies controlled much of Peru's natural resources. These companies developed new industries, but they

Government

According to the country's laws, Peru is to be governed by elected leaders. There were times when people were not allowed to vote for their leaders, especially when the army controlled the government from 1949 to 1956 and again from 1968 to 1980. In 1980, Peruvians were finally able to elect their leaders again and a new **constitution** came into effect. Today, the biggest problem the government faces is poverty, unemployment, terrorism, and crime.

Simon Bolivar, a general from Venezuela, helped many South American countries, including Peru, gain independence from Spain.

In 1996, the terrorist group MTRA took hostages at the Japanese embassy in Lima. The military rescued all but one of the hostages and killed the terrorists.

him support in Peru. Terrorist activity declined and Fujimori was president until 2000. He resigned in 2001, when he was accused of corruption. He now lives in Japan.

Looking ahead

Peru still faces many challenges, but there is hope for a better future. Terrorist groups are losing strength, violence is declining, and the problems of indigenous people living in poverty has been brought to the attention of Peru's president, Alejandro Toledo, who is himself of indigenous descent.

Terrorism

The Shining Path is a terrorist group that operates in Peru. Terrorists are people who try to achieve their political goals using violence. The Shining Path was formed in 1980. For years it fought to overthrow the government with bombings and murders. The government was harsh in its attempts to stop the Shining Path. Innocent people were often caught in the middle. If they sided with the government, the Shining Path might harm them or their families, and if they sided with the Shining Path, they might face going to jail.

Another terrorist group in Peru is the Tupac Amaru Revolutionary Movement (MTRA). They took over the residence of the Japanese ambassador in December 1996. The siege gained them attention but ended when President Alberto Fujimori sent in the military, who killed the terrorists.

Alberto Fujimori

In 1990, Alberto Fujimori was elected president of Peru. One of his first tasks was to deal with the terrorist groups that threatened the country and **corruption** within the government. In 1992, Fujimori made a decision to put Peru's constitution on hold and to run the country without elected officials. This allowed him to put leaders of terrorist groups in jail and won

In April 2001, Alejandro Toledo was elected Peru's first indigenous president. Many Peruvians hope Toledo will focus on the issue of poverty among Peru's indigenous peoples.

The Peruvians

About half of the population of Peru is made up of indigenous, or Native, peoples who speak either **Quechua**, the language of the Incas, or Aymara. Only about one tenth of Peruvians are descended from Spanish or Europeans settlers, and the rest are a mix of Spanish and indigenous people.

Indigenas

There are about nine million indigenous peoples, or *indigenas*, in Peru. Indigenous peoples are the original inhabitants of an area. Over half of Peru's *indigenas* speak Aymara or Quechua languages. Most of Peru's indigenous peoples live in the highlands and along the coast. A much smaller number live in the rainforests. Highland indigenous peoples live at altitudes up to 15,000 feet (4,570 meters) in the Andes mountains. Almost all highlanders work as farmers.

European descent

Explorers from Spain were the first Europeans to arrive in Peru. The Spanish sailed from Europe in the 1520s, searching for gold and other treasures. They fought with the Inca for control over the land. After many years of fighting, the Spanish defeated the Inca civilization and conquered Peru. The Spanish began a period of **colonization** which included building new cities and **imposing** Spanish laws and religion on the indigenous people. Today, people of European ancestry, or *criollos*, such as the Spanish, make up about ten percent of Peru's population.

(both) Peru's indigenous people make up about half the population of the country. Indigenous peoples live in the mountain highlands, along the coast, and in the rainforests of Peru.

Mixed ancestry

After the Spanish conquest of Peru, some Spaniards and indigenous peoples married. Their descendants are called *mestizos* by Peruvians of European descent and *mistikuna* by the Quechua people, who are descended from the Inca. Today, it is estimated that approximately 43 percent of all Peruvians are *mestizos*. *Mestizos* speak Spanish and wear Western-style clothing. Historically, *mestizos* worked as supervisors for the European owners of mines and plantations. Today, many *mestizos* have become leaders in government, industry, the armed forces, and other professions traditionally held only by Peruvians of European descent.

Other Peruvians

Peru also has a small number of people of African, Chinese, and Japanese descent. Most African-Peruvians are descended from the slaves brought to Peru by the Spanish in the 1500s. Slavery was abolished in Peru in the mid-1800s. The Chinese came as **indentured** laborers to build the Andean railway in the 1800s.

(above) On the Uros Islands in Lake Titicaca, the people live traditional lives, isolated from most other Peruvians.

(below) In the highland villages of the Andes mountains, Quechua families still farm and herd llamas, much as their Inca ancestors did.

City life

Peru's cities look very different today than they did a generation ago. Over the last three decades, people from the mountain highlands and rural areas flocked to the cities in search of employment and better living conditions. Many people fled to escape the terrorist activities of the Shining Path and the government's military operations to stop them. Today, over 70 percent of Peru's population lives in busy cities such as Lima and Arequipa, which are both located along the Pacific coast.

City homes

In Peru's cities, there are very poor and very rich neighborhoods. For those who can afford to live in a good home, life is comfortable. In the Miraflores suburb of Lima, large, beautiful homes are built in both Spanish colonial and modern styles. There are many parks and private schools for children, restaurants to eat in, and shops filled with the latest products. Houses have running water, electricity, and televisions, and people in Miraflores have cars.

(above) Children playing in the **pueblos jovenes,** *or "young towns," on the outskirts of the city of Lima.*

(below) The Miraflores suburb in Lima, is a wealthy neighborhood with large homes, parks, and shopping districts.

(above) A father and son enjoy an afternoon in one of the parks of Lima's Miraflores district.

(right) Costumed students from Quillabamba school protest the deforestation of the rainforest.

The *barrida*

The poorest urban area is the shanty town, or *barrida*, on the hills outside of Lima. Since the late 1960s, this *barrida* has also been known as the *pueblos jovenes*, or "young town." About one million people live there, many of whom arrived with their families from the highland villages in search of employment and a better life.

Many of the people who live in the *barrida* are unemployed and suffer terrible poverty. Houses have no electricity or indoor plumbing, and there are no schools or hospitals in the *barrida*. In recent years some sewers and water lines have been added to the *barrida* by Peru's government, but unsanitary conditions and crime remain serious problems for the people who live in this area.

Going to school

Peru has an education system that takes eleven years to complete. The pre-primary level is for children up to age six. The second level is called the primary level, and is for ages six to fifteen. Finally a five-year secondary level begins at age twelve. Education is free and children must attend until age sixteen, but the government has difficulty enforcing this rule in rural areas. Less than 59 percent of school age children attend school regularly. One reason is that many children must work to help support their families instead of going to school. Some children work as street vendors selling handmade jewelry to tourists in downtown Lima.

Employment

Peru's cities are crowded with people looking for work. Unfortunately, only a few find jobs. Others have jobs but receive very low pay for their work. Peru's government does not have enough money to help all the people who are unemployed or underpaid. Some people hope that foreign companies will create jobs by building businesses and factories in Peru. Others worry foreign companies will take more out of Peru than they bring in.

Village life

Thousands of small towns, villages, and hamlets are scattered throughout Peru. From the valleys and plateaus of the Andes mountains, to isolated pockets in the Amazon rainforest, the majority of Peruvian villages are populated by indigenous peoples.

Mountain villages

The fertile valleys and high plateaus of the Andes mountains are home to small villages and hamlets where approximately 36 percent of the population of Peru lives. These highlanders live in sturdy homes, constructed with stones or **adobe** bricks to protect them from the winds and cold temperatures. The roofs are made of straw or ichu grass. Most highlanders earn a living by farming. In recent years, many highlanders have left their homes for the city, in search of jobs and better lives for their families.

Rainforest villages

In Peru's rainforest region, or *selva*, groups of indigenous peoples live in clusters at the edges of rivers, such as the Amazon. Groups such as the Shipibo, Ashaninka, and Aguaruna lived here quite isolated from the rest of Peru until the mid-1900s.

(above) Villages dot the shores of Lake Titicaca high in the Andes mountains of southern Peru.

(below) On the waters of Lake Titicaca, on the border with Bolivia, the Uros people use the plentiful totora reeds that grow in the lake to weave their homes and other buildings, such as this chapel.

(above) A Machiguenga settlement at Tayakuma and the Manu River. Many families in the Amazon share one large house.

(above) These houses are built atop supports that keep them from flooding during heavy rains. The floors are made of hardwoods that discourage insects from chewing through. On hot days, cool breezes blow through the window spaces.

(below) Squatters set up a home in the desert outside of Arequipa. Desert homes are constructed of materials such as clay, straw, and stones.

The indigenous peoples of the *selva* depend on fishing, hunting, and gathering from the forest for their livelihood. They farm following an ancient system known as slash-and-burn. In slash-and-burn farming a plot of land is farmed for only a three to five year period. It is then abandoned and the farmers move on to farm another area. This practice allows the vegetation and thin soil to recuperate and the farmer can use it again in ten years.

Desert villages

Humans have lived for over 10,000 years in the larger coastal valley oases of Peru. The largest of these oases became religious centers and important cities of ancient civilizations. Today, modern towns and cities are on these sites. People living along the coast fish and hunt on the shoreline. They also farm using irrigation systems. Throughout the coastal valleys, villages remain dependent on the waters flowing from the Andes mountains along canals and aqueducts first built 3,000 years ago.

Religion and festivals

The constitution of Peru guarantees freedom of religion to all citizens. About 90 percent of Peruvians are Roman Catholic, a **denomination** of Christianity headed by the Pope in Rome. Christianity is a religion based on the teachings of Jesus Christ, who Christians believe was the son of God on Earth. Today, most indigenous peoples blend their ancient religious customs with Catholic beliefs.

Roman Catholicism

The Spanish brought Roman Catholicism to Peru in the 1500s and forced many indigenous peoples to follow its practices. Spanish **missionaries** worked to convert the indigenous peoples to Catholicism by replacing their local gods with Christian **saints** and building churches on top of their temples. Peruvian children are still taught Roman Catholicism in schools today.

Catholic and Inca beliefs

Most Peruvians are Roman Catholics, but many indigenous people still practice traditional religions and worship Inca gods. The ancient Incas built mountaintop sites to worship the sun and mountains. Today, indigenous people continue to honor the mountains. Before beginning a journey through the Andes, travelers make an offering of statues, coca leaves, incense, and llama fat. These offerings are sold in the village markets in bundles called *despachos*.

Amazon magic

Some indigenous people in the Amazon rainforest believe in the powers of **shamans**. Shamans use the bark of a vine to brew a potion called *ayahuasca*. After drinking *ayahuasca*, shamans believe they can travel in space or time and transform themselves into animals such as jaguars and anacondas. Most shamans use their skills for healing and protecting people.

(above) Almost every town or village in Peru holds an annual fair, or feria, where colorful processions, feasting, music, and dancing take place.

Protestantism

In recent decades, many Protestant denominations, such as Pentecostalism and **Mormonism**, have become popular in Peru. Protestants are Christians who place less value on religious ceremony than on the word of God in the Bible. Protestant missionaries converted many Peruvians who were unhappy with Roman Catholicism. Indigenous Peruvians and poor people living in the cities felt Catholicism had not succeeded in helping them deal with the problems they face, such as poverty.

Fiestas and *ferias*

Peruvians celebrate their religious heritage with lively festivals called *fiestas*. Fiesta means "feast day" in the Spanish language. During *fiestas*, families and friends gather late into the night to eat, drink, and enjoy one another's company. Almost every town and village holds an annual fair, or *feria*, to honor its **patron** saint. *Ferias* include colorful religious **processions**, feasting, dancing, and games.

The Lord of the Miracles

The most important and largest religious festival in Peru takes place in October. The Lord of the Miracles festival gathers together the largest number of believers in South America. The heart of the celebration is a procession of tens of thousands of people who dress in purple tunics, sing hymns, and pray as they accompany a painted image of Jesus Christ through the streets of Lima. Many Peruvians believe this image is **holy**.

The Feast of *Corpus Christi*

An important festival in the mountain region of Peru takes place every year at the end of June. During the Feast of *Corpus Christi*, people from surrounding areas come to the city of Cuzco for eight days. Statues of saints, which are housed in the churches of Cuzco, are honored and dressed in beautiful costumes. On the eighth day of the festival, a procession is held. Musicians, dancers, and other participants parade through the city streets.

Inti Raymi

Inti Raymi is an ancient Inca sun-worshipping festival that celebrates the middle of Peru's winter and the end of the harvest. During the Inti Raymi festival, which is held on June 24, brightly costumed performers dance and offer gifts of food to Inti, the sun god, in thanks for warmth and light he provides.

(above) During the Inti Raymi festival in Cuzco, performers dressed in costumes of ancient Inca design dance and offer gifts of food to Inti, the sun god, in thanks for the warmth and light he provides.

(below) The procession at the festival of Our Lord of the Miracles through the streets of Lima follows a painted image of Jesus Christ that survived an earthquake in 1746.

Sports and leisure

Peruvians enjoy many sports and leisure activities. Some sports, such as soccer and bullfighting were brought to Peru by the Spanish hundred of years ago. Newer sports such as volleyball, tennis, horseracing, and basketball have been borrowed from other countries and are growing in popularity.

Soccer

Peruvians love to play and watch soccer, which they call *futbol*. The National Stadium, or Estadio Nacional, in Lima, holds 45,000 people and is always crowded during games. Every four years, countries around the world compete in the World Cup Games to determine the international soccer champions. When the Peruvian national team plays, there is much excitement as people gather around televisions and radios to watch and listen to the games.

Fighting the bulls

Bullfighting was introduced to Peru by the Spanish in the 1500s. Every October and November, bullfights take place in Lima's Plaza de Acho, the oldest and largest bullfighting ring in South America. A bullfighter, or *torero*, swirls a red cape around his or her shoulders. The movement of the cape enrages the bull into charging at the bullfighter, who leaps gracefully from the bull's path just in time to escape its horns. Eventually, the bull is killed because it is too tired to fight. Some people consider bullfighting a cruel sport and are working to get it stopped.

(top) Soccer, or **futbol**, *is Peru's national sport and is played all over the country by people of all ages.*

(opposite) The Plaza de Acho in Lima is the oldest bullfighting ring in South America.

Music and dance

Music and dance have been important parts of Peru's cultural life for 10,000 years. There are about 1,300 musical styles in Peru, from the folk music of Inca origin, which today combines many cultural influences, to new styles such as *chicha*, which is a fusion of Colombian dance with Andean music. *Chicha* is especially popular in the *pueblos jovenes*. The two most common musical styles in Peru are the coastal and highland. The *criolla*, or coastal style, is energetic and merry, whereas the highland, or *andina* style, is often slow and mournful.

Ancient instruments

Traditional instruments are still used to produce age-old melodies. The *quena*, which is similar to a flute and often made from an animal bone, has been played for over 2,000 years. Several pipes of different sizes make up the *antara*, while the *bombo leguero* is a huge drum constructed from willow and goat skin. The *charango* is like a small guitar, but with one difference - its body is made from the shell of an armadillo!

Dancing

Dancing makes celebrations even more festive in Peru and there are many regional styles of dance. The *marinera* is a dance performed at *fiestas* in the coastal region. Guitar strumming and lively singing provide background music for a pretend **courtship**, which is acted out by couples waving colored handkerchiefs. In the mountains, there are over 200 different kinds of dances performed by the indigenous peoples living there. One dance is called the *huaynito serrano*, in which dancers repeat slow, skipping steps over and over. This sad-looking dance is accompanied by the music of a harp and *quena*. In the cities, people gather to dance in *peñas*, where folk music, jazz, and Peruvian Creole, a music that combines European musical forms with native Peruvian, Spanish, and African rhythms and instruments, is played.

(opposite, top) Traditional Peruvian dance is performed as part of a fiesta.

*(opposite, bottom) Musicians playing traditional **zamponas** at the Manco Capac fiesta in Puno give Andean music a haunting sound. Zamponas are a type of pan flute.*

(above) A Peruvian musician plays the charango, a guitar-like instrument sometimes made from the shell of an armadillo.

(below) Many blind people in Peru make a living by playing music on the streets of large cities and towns.

Arts and language

Long before the Spanish arrived, the ancient civilizations of Peru had established an impressive artistic heritage. The Moche, Nazca, and Inca cultures all painted intricate designs on pottery, and were skilled weavers and architects, decorating their temples with colorful **friezes**. When the Spanish arrived in the 1530s and conquered the Inca, they quickly began decorating newly-built churches and houses with art influenced by Christianity.

The Lima and Cuzco schools

Several schools, or styles, of painting soon emerged in Peru. In 1574, an Italian artist named Bernado Bitti came to Lima to set up art schools. Bitti used the Bible as a major source of inspiration. Bitti eventually had schools in Cuzco, Puno, and La Paz, where his students painted colorful and uplifting scenes of religious and holy people. The style of painting Bitti introduced is now called the Lima School.

In the 1700s, another major school of Peruvian art emerged. The Cuzco School, named after the city where many of its artists lived, is also religious in origin. Students painted Roman Catholic saints in the image of indigenous Peruvians. Artists also used gold dust in their paintings to give the work a distinctive look.

(top) An example of a mural by a Cuzco School artist, Tadeo Escalante, in the Huaro Church near Cuzco. The mural was painted in the 1700s.

(left) An open air exhibit by Cuzco artists, in Miraflores, Lima.

Indigenism

An artistic and literary movement called Indigenism became popular in Peru in the 1920s. Led by a woodcarver named Jose Sabogal, Indigenism celebrates the culture and heritage of Peru's indigenous peoples. The most famous Indigenist artist was Jorge Vihatea Reynoso. Sculptors, writers, wall artists called muralists, and other artists all use their talents to express their pride in indigenous culture.

Literature

There was no written language in Peru before the Spanish arrived, but after the 1530s a rich body of literature began to develop out of the traditional stories that had been passed down orally for centuries in Peru. A popular colonial writer was Garcilaso de la Vega, who recorded the last days of the Inca Empire. The first independent literary movement in Peru was known as *costumbrismo*, and centered around condemning the Spanish past and glorifying the Quechua culture. Ricardo Palma was a notable *costumbrismo* writer. The most celebrated Peruvian poet was Cesar Vallejo, who wrote his poems in a realistic style and was very interested in social causes. In recent years, a generation of women writers, such as Carmen Olle, Maria Emilio Cornejo, and Giovanna Pollarola has also emerged in Peru.

(top) Famous Peruvian writer Mario Vargas Llosa.

Mario Vargas Llosa

One of the world's most respected writers was born in Arequipa, in the southern part of Peru. Mario Vargas Llosa worked as a journalist and a professor before becoming a novelist. Most of Llosa's novels are set in Peru and deal with the harsh realities of Peru's social and political life. His outspoken written attacks on political corruption, racial prejudices, and violence have made him a controversial figure in his home country while earning him popularity abroad. In 1990 he ran for president and lost in a close election to Alberto Fujimori.

Learn to speak Quechua

Quechua is the language of the ancient Inca Empire and is still spoken by about 10 million people in the Cuzco region of southern Peru. In 1975, Quechua became Peru's second official language, after Spanish. Here are a few phrases for you to try.

English	Quechua	Spanish
Hello	*Napaykullaki*	*Buenos dias*
How are you?	*Allillanchu?*	*Como esta usted?*
Thanks	*Anay*	*Gracias*
Yes	*Ari*	*Si*
No	*Mana*	*No*
Goodbye	*Kacharpari*	*Aios*

Clothing

Traditional clothing

In rural areas of Peru, the Quechua people wear a blend of traditional Inca clothing and European fashions. Quechua girls and women wear several layers of long, handwoven skirts. These skirts are usually black but they are decorated with bright, colorful trim. Women wrap a short cape, or *lliclla*, around their shoulders or draped over their heads. Brightly-colored petticoats, known as *polleras*, are variations of the long wrap-around gowns traditionally worn by Inca women. Men wear a shirt, vest, or coat over calf-length black trousers with a brightly-colored sash sometimes knotted at the waist. In the mountain region, a *poncho* or *serape* provides warmth on chilly nights. The *poncho* is pulled over the head, whereas the *serape* opens at the front, like a jacket.

The arts of weaving and dyeing fabric have been passed down from generation to generation for hundreds of years in Peru. These arts are still used in making traditional clothing among Peru's indigenous peoples. Colonial Spanish clothing has also influenced Peruvian fashions. Most people wear modern clothing in their daily lives, but traditional and Spanish costumes are often worn at festivals and on special occasions.

(top) Aymara men on the Island of Taquile in the Lake Titicaca region knit their own woolen caps.

(right) A Yagua shaman from the Amazon rainforest wears a traditional dress of palm fiber.

In the mountains, woolen or straw hats are also part of the traditional dress. In the coldest parts of the Andes, highlanders wear a *chullo*, a woolen cap fitted with earflaps and decorated with geometric figures. In the jungle, some men and women wear a *cushma*, a loose tunic stitched up on both sides and decorated with dyes and geometric figures.

The *caballero*

Some Peruvians still put on traditional Spanish-colonial costumes for special occasions. The men wear a *caballero*, or cowboy, outfit. A short velvet jacket, called a *bolero*, is worn over a fine white shirt made of silk or satin. Tight velvet breeches match the *bolero*. *Chaparajos*, or chaps, go over the breeches and are **ornamented** with fancy white and black braids. A black felt hat and black leather boots complete this costume. The women dress in an fringed shawl over a white satin gown. A lace *mantilla* is draped over her hair and held in place by a fancy comb.

(above) A young girl drapes a black **liclla**, *or short shawl, over her head. On cold days, hats are worn over the* **liclla**.

(right) Layers of embroidered skirts and a colorful vest contrast with modern track pants and running shoes. A traditional pouch worn at the waist holds this young woman's spinning tools and wool.

A taste of Peru

Food is an important part of Peru's culture. Over the centuries, ancient Inca **staples** such as maize, or corn, potatoes, and chilies have been combined with Spanish ingredients to create great-tasting regional dishes. In big cities, such as Lima, Peruvian cuisine has become a multicultural blend of flavors, influenced by the ingredients of the people of Chinese, European, African, and Japanese ancestry who live there.

Ancient cuisine

One of the most important ingredients during Inca times was maize, or corn. The Incas prepared maize by toasting it or boiling it in water. On special occasions, maize was made into bread and *humitas*, or tamales. Another basic food for the Incas was the potato. The Incas living high in the Andes mountains grew a wide variety of potatoes, which they cooked or roasted and used to make hearty stews.

(above) **Ceviche** *is a traditional Peruvian meal of cold seafood and vegetables. Here it is served with rice.*

(below) Roasted guinea pig, or **cuy,** *is a delicacy found in many parts of Peru. The skin is of the guinea pig is often dried and cut to make* **charqui,** *which is used in soups and stews.*

Andean meals

The ingredients and styles of Peruvian meals differ from region to region. In the mountain highlands of the Andes, for instance, the most typical dish is *pachamanca*, which is cooked in a hole in the ground over hot stones. Ingredients include green beans, potatoes, corn, and several types of meat seasoned with herbs and spices. Soup dishes include *pucheros*, *patasca*, and *caldo de cabeza de cordero*, or sheep's head broth, which are favorites when it gets cold. Beef is often freeze-dried into *charqui*, while *cuy*, or guinea pig, is served in a variety of sauces and stews. Irresistible dishes include *papa a la huancaína*, or potato in a spicy cheese sauce. In the southern Arequipa highlands such dishes as *rocoto relleno*, or stuffed chili peppers, and *cordero al horno*, or roast lamb, are very popular.

(left) Masses of **aji**, *or chili peppers, on the ground drying near Casma. Aji was originally called "uchu" by the Incas and it was known as "pepper from the Indies" by the Spanish. Today,* **aji** *is the most important seasoning used to prepare meals in Peruvian kitchen.*

(below) Quechua women enjoy a refreshing glass of **chicha** *at an outdoor harvest festival.*

Corn beer

Chicha is a Peruvian corn beer that has been brewed since ancient times. The Incas drank *chicha* during religious festivals. The brew was served from specially painted or engraved beakers called *keros*. Today, people enjoy *chicha* any day of the year. It tastes bitter when **fermented**. Unfermented, it is a delicious nonalcoholic beverage. Businesses that specialize in brewing *chicha* have red flags hanging over their doors.

Rainforest meals

The indigenous peoples of the rainforest hunt and eat a wide variety of animals, such as tapirs, wild pigs, rabbits, and monkeys. Doves, partridges, and wild turkeys provide poultry meat. A dry, salted fish called *paiche* is a popular dish. Tree sap is a light, refreshing drink. *Masato* and *canazo* are alcoholic beverages made from fermented plants and fruit.

Coastal meals

Fishing has always been an important source of food for Peruvians living along the coast. Coastal Peruvians also eat llama, duck, and in certain areas dog. Guinea pig is also eaten along the coast. The skin of the guinea pig is dried and later chopped to make *charqui*. *Charqui* is used to prepare soups and stews.

Spanish influence

After the arrival of the Spanish in the 1530s, a number of ingredients and culinary styles from Europe and the rest of the world were brought to Peru. This process was known as *mestizaje*. Among these new ingredients were cows, hens, and rabbits. Wheat was also introduced but it took three years before it was actually used to make bread. Vegetables such as lettuce, eggplant, onions, spinach, asparagus, and fruits such as figs, oranges, limes, peaches, apples, and cherries, were also brought from Europe, along with the important contribution of sugar cane. Sugar cane was used to make desserts during the colonial period. During this time, many Spanish recipes began to incorporate Peruvian ingredients such as maize, yams, potatoes, yucca, and bananas.

Oriental influence

Between 1849 and 1874, nearly 100,000 Chinese immigrants arrived in Peru to work as laborers on the Andean railway. After this migration, the *fondas,* or places where the Chinese used to eat, began to appear around Chinese neighborhoods in cities such as Lima. There are now over 2,000 Chinese restaurants, or *chifas,* in Peru and every grocery market carries a selection of Chinese ingredients along with local ingredients and seafood from Peru's Pacific coast.

Eating out

Peruvians living in big cities sometimes go out to restaurants for lunch or on special occasions, usually to a *cevicheria.* This kind of restaurant serves a wide variety of seafood. *Ceviche* is the most traditional meal in Peru. It is served cold and consists mainly of pieces of cold fish cooked in lemon juice. There are many variations but it is always served with onions, *camote,* a sweet Peruvian potato, and *aji* peppers.

(left) A woman sells **pitajaya,** *an edible cactus fruit, at the highland market of Chachapoyas.*

(opposite) Fishers distribute the day's catch at Puerto Eden, on the coast.

Natillas piuranas

Natillas piuranas is a very sweet milk pudding, and is a favorite dessert in Peru and other South America countries. It has many names, such as *manjar blanco, dulce de leche,* and *leche quemada.* This recipe serves six to eight people. Ask an adult for help when using the stove.

3 cups (750 ml) milk
1 3/4 cups (450 ml) condensed milk
1/2 tsp (2.5 ml) baking soda
1 cup (250 ml) dark-brown sugar
1/4 cup (60 ml) water

In a small saucepan over high heat, bring the milk, condensed milk, and baking soda to a boil, while stirring constantly. Remove pan from heat. Combine the sugar and water in a large, heavy saucepan and cook over low heat, stirring until the sugar dissolves. Add the hot milk mixture and stir well. Cook over low heat for 75 minutes. Stir occasionally. The mixture will become a thick, amber-colored pudding. Serve at room temperature or refrigerate and serve chilled. To add color and flavor, you can sprinkle the pudding lightly with cinnamon.

Glossary

adobe Brick made of clay and straw that is dried in the sun

archaeology The study of buildings and artifacts from the past

colonial Relating to a territory ruled by or belonging to another nation

constitution The basic laws and principles under which a country is governed

corruption The act of being dishonest in business or politics

courtship The act of trying to win the love of another in order to marry

culture The customs, beliefs, and arts of a distinct group of people

denomination An organized religious group within a faith

divert To change the course or direction

ferment To change the sugar in a liquid to alcohol and a gas through a chemical process

frieze An ancient wall painting

holy Having to do with the worship of God or a divine being

impose To force to accept

indenture A contract binding one person into the service of another for a period of time

irrigation The process of bringing water to the land, so that crops can grow

missionary A person sent to a foreign land to spread religion and do good works

Mormanism A religious denomination based on the teachings of the Bible and the Book of Morman

myth A legend or story that explains mysterious events or ideas

oases Areas in a desert that are fertile because of the presence of water

ornamented Decorated or made more beautiful

patron A person who supports or helps another person, an activity, or institution

procession A group of persons or vehicles moving along in an orderly, formal manner

Quechua The language and name of a South American indigenous group descended from the Inca

saint A person through whom God has performed miracles, according to the Christian church

shaman A person who uses magic to cure illness and control spiritual forces

staple A main product that is grown or produced in a region

Index

1 2 3 4 5 6 7 8 9 0 Printed in the USA 0 9 8 7 6 5 4 3 2